The Happy Prince

Oscar Wilde
Illustrated by Tracie Grimwood

CELEBRATION PRESS
Pearson Learning Group

High above the city, on a tall column, stood the statue of the Happy Prince. He was gilded all over with thin leaves of fine gold, for eyes he had two bright sapphires, and a large red ruby glowed on his sword-hilt.

He was very much admired indeed.

"Why can't you be like the Happy Prince?" a mother asked her little boy. "The Happy Prince never dreams of crying about anything."

One night there flew over the city a little Swallow. He saw the statue on the tall column and landed just between the feet of the Happy Prince. He prepared to go to sleep; but just as he was putting his head under his wing, a large drop of water fell on him. Then another drop fell. A third drop fell, and he looked up.

The eyes of the Happy Prince were filled with tears, and tears were running down his golden cheeks. His face was so beautiful in the moonlight that the little Swallow was filled with pity.

"Who are you?" he said.

"I am the Happy Prince."

"Why are you weeping then?" asked the Swallow. "You have quite drenched me."

"When I was alive and had a human heart," answered the statue, "I did not know what tears were. My courtiers called me the Happy Prince, and happy indeed I was. And now that I am dead, they have set me here so high that I can see all the misery of my city, and though my heart is made of lead, I cannot choose but weep."

"Far away," continued the statue, "is a poor house. In a bed a little boy is lying ill. He is asking for oranges. His mother has nothing to give him but river water, so he is crying. Swallow, Swallow, little Swallow, will you not bring her the ruby out of my sword-hilt?"

“I am waited for in Egypt,” said the Swallow. “My friends are flying up and down the Nile, and talking to the large lotus flowers.”

“Swallow, Swallow, little Swallow,” said the Prince, “will you not stay with me for one night, and be my messenger? The boy is so thirsty, and the mother so sad.”

The Happy Prince looked so sad that the little Swallow was sorry.

“I will stay with you for one night, and be your messenger.”

He picked out the great ruby from the Prince's sword, and flew away with it in his beak over the roofs of the town.

He passed by the cathedral tower, where the white marble angels were sculpted. He passed over the river, and saw the lanterns hanging on the masts of the ships. At last he came to the poor house where the little boy lay ill and dropped the ruby onto the table.

Then he flew back to the Happy Prince, and told him what he had done. “It is curious, but I feel quite warm now, although it is so cold.”

“That is because you have done a good deed,” said the Prince.

When the moon rose the next day the Swallow looked up at the Happy Prince. "I am just starting for Egypt," he said.

"Swallow, Swallow, little Swallow," said the Prince, "will you not stay with me one night longer?"

"I am waited for in Egypt," answered the Swallow. "At noon the yellow lions come down to the water's edge to drink. They have eyes like green bells."

"Swallow, Swallow, little Swallow," said the Prince, "far away across the city I see a young man in an attic. He is trying to finish a play for the Director of the Theater, but he is too cold to write any more. There is no fire in the hearth, and hunger has made him faint."

"I will wait with you one night longer," said the Swallow, who really had a good heart. "Shall I take him another ruby?"

"Alas! I have no ruby now," said the Prince. "My eyes are all that I have left. They are made of rare sapphires. Pluck one of them out and take it to him."

"Dear Prince," said the Swallow, "I cannot do that," and he began to weep.

"Swallow, Swallow, little Swallow," said the Prince, "do as I command you."

So the Swallow plucked out the Prince's eye and flew away to the student's attic. When the student looked up he found the sapphire lying on his desk.

“I must bid you goodbye,” cried the Swallow, when the moon rose the next night. “I am going to Egypt!”

“Swallow, Swallow, little Swallow,” said the Prince, “will you not stay with me one night longer?”

"It is winter," answered the Swallow, "and the snow will soon be here. In Egypt the sun is warm on the palm trees, and the crocodiles lie in the mud and look lazily about them. Dear Prince, I must leave you, but next spring I will bring you back two beautiful jewels in place of those you have given away."

"In the square below," said the Happy Prince, "there stands a little match girl. She has let her matches fall in the gutter. She is crying. She has no shoes or stockings, and her little head is bare. Pluck out my other eye, and give it to her."

"I will stay with you one night longer," said the Swallow, "but I cannot pluck out your eye. You would be quite blind then."

"Swallow, Swallow, little Swallow," said the Prince, "do as I command you."

So the Swallow plucked out the Prince's other eye, darted down with it and slipped the jewel right into the palm of the little match girl's hand.

Then the Swallow came back to the Prince. "You are blind now," he said, "so I will stay with you always."

"No, little Swallow," said the poor Prince, "you must go away to Egypt."

"I will stay with you always," said the Swallow, and he slept at the Prince's feet.

All the next day he sat on the Prince's shoulder and told him stories of what he had seen in strange lands. He told him of the red ibises, who stand in long rows on the banks of the Nile and catch goldfish in their beaks.

He told him of the Sphinx, who is as old as the world itself and lives in the desert and knows everything.

And of the great green snake that sleeps in a palm tree.

"Dear little Swallow," said the Prince, "you tell me of marvelous things, but there is no mystery so great as misery. Fly over my city, little Swallow, and tell me what you see there."

So the Swallow flew over the great city and saw the rich merrymaking in their beautiful houses while the beggars were standing at the gates. He saw the white faces of starving children looking out at the black streets. Then he flew back and told the Prince what he had seen.

"I am covered with fine gold," said the Prince. "You must take it off, leaf by leaf, and give it to the poor."

Leaf after leaf of the fine gold the Swallow picked off, until the Happy Prince looked quite dull and gray. Leaf after leaf of the fine gold he brought to the poor, and the children's faces grew rosier, and they laughed and played games in the street. "We have bread now!" they cried.

Then the snow came, and after the snow came the frost. Everybody went about in furs, and the little boys wore scarlet caps and skated on the ice.

The poor little Swallow grew colder and colder, but he would not leave the Prince. He loved him too well.

But at last he knew he was going to die. "Goodbye, dear Prince!" he murmured. And he kissed the Happy Prince and fell down dead at his feet.

At that moment a curious crack sounded inside the statue. The leaden heart had snapped right in two.

Early the next morning the Mayor was walking in the square below with the town councilmen. "Dear me! How shabby the Happy Prince looks!" he said. "There is actually a dead bird at his feet!" he continued.

They pulled down the statue of the Happy Prince. Then they melted the statue in a furnace. But the broken lead heart would not melt, so it was thrown on a dust heap, where the dead Swallow was also laying.

“Bring me the two most precious things in the city,” said God to one of his angels; and the angel brought him the leaden heart and the dead bird.

“You have chosen rightly,” said God, “for in my garden of Paradise this little bird shall sing, and the Happy Prince shall live forever more.”